A teacher is a very special person
who uses his or her creativity
and loving, inquiring mind
to develop the rare talent
of encouraging others to think,
 to dream, to learn, to try, to do!

– Beverly Conklin

TEACHING

and
Learning
Are Lifelong
Journeys

*Thoughts on the Art of Teaching
and the Meaning of Education*

A Collection from Blue Mountain Arts®

The publisher wishes to acknowledge and thank Tania Lombrozo for her extensive help in compiling the poems and quotations in this collection.

Library of Congress Catalog Card Number: 99-15442
ISBN: 0-88396-519-4

ACKNOWLEDGMENTS appear on page 48.

M design on book cover is registered in the U.S. Patent and Trademark Office.

Manufactured in the United States of America
First Printing: May 1999

✪ This book is printed on recycled paper.

Library of Congress Cataloging-in-Publication Data

Teaching and learning are lifelong journeys : thoughts on the art of
  teaching and the meaning of education : a collection from Blue
  Mountain Arts.
      p.   cm.
    ISBN 0-88396-519-4 (alk. paper)
    1. Teaching Quotations, maxims, etc. I. Blue Mountain Arts
  (Firm) II. Title: Thoughts on the art of teaching and the meaning
  of education.
  LB 1775.T4187   1999
  371.1'002--dc21
                                                    99-15442
                                                       CIP

Blue Mountain Press INC.

P.O. Box 4549, Boulder, Colorado 80306

Contents

(Authors listed in order of first appearance)

What Is a Teacher?

A teacher is someone
   who sees each child
as a unique person
and encourages individual
   talents and strengths.

A teacher looks beyond
   each child's face
and sees inside their souls.

A teacher is someone
   with a special touch
and a ready smile
who takes the time
to listen to both sides
and always tries to be fair.

A teacher has a caring heart
that respects and understands.

A teacher is someone
who can look past disruption
   and rebellion,
and recognize hurt and pain.

A teacher teaches the entire child
and helps to build confidence
   and raise self-esteem.

A teacher makes a difference
   in each child's life
and affects each family
and the future of us all.

— Barbara Cage

It is noble to teach oneself; it is still nobler to teach others.

— Mark Twain

To live a single day and hear a good teaching is better than to live a hundred years without knowing such teaching.

— Buddha

I touch the future, I teach.

— Christa McAuliffe

It is the supreme art of the teacher
to awaken joy in creative expression
and knowledge.

— Albert Einstein

Not only is there an art in knowing a
thing, but also a certain art in teaching it.

— Marcus Tullius Cicero

The one exclusive sign of a thorough
knowledge is the power of teaching.

— Aristotle

One looks back with appreciation to the brilliant teachers, but with gratitude to those who touched our human feelings. The curriculum is so much necessary raw material, but warmth is the vital element for the growing plant and for the soul of the child.

– Carl Gustav Jung

A teacher affects eternity; he can never tell where his influence stops.

– Henry Brooks Adams

Knowledge is power.

– Francis Bacon

A teacher should know more than he teaches, and if he knows more than he teaches, he will teach more than he knows.

– Anonymous

What the teacher is, is more important than what he teaches.

– Karl Menninger

In seeking knowledge, the first step is silence, the second listening, the third remembering, the fourth practicing, and the fifth — teaching others.

— Solomon Ibn Gabirol

Teaching is one of the most crucial, responsible and important professions — since it consists of communicating knowledge and guiding the intellectual development of men. The objective purpose of teaching is the spread and communication of the right ideas, of intellectual values, which means: the creation of a culture.

— Ayn Rand

To know how to suggest is the great art of teaching.

— Henri Frédéric Amiel

How to tell students what to look for without telling them what to see is the dilemma of teaching.

— Lascelles Abercrombie

No man can reveal to you aught but that which already lies half asleep in the dawning of your knowledge.

The teacher who walks in the shadow of the temple, among his followers, gives not of his wisdom but rather of his faith and his lovingness.

If he is indeed wise he does not bid you enter the house of his wisdom, but rather leads you to the threshold of your own mind.

— Kahlil Gibran

The good teacher, the proper teacher, must be ever-living in faith and ever-renewed in creative energy to keep the sap packed in herself, himself, as well as the work.

— Sylvia Plath

It is a general insight, which merits more attention than it receives, that teaching should not be compared to filling a bottle with water but rather to helping a flower to grow in its own way. As any good teacher knows, the methods of instruction and the range of material covered are matters of small importance as compared with the success in arousing the natural curiosity of the students and stimulating their interest in exploring on their own.

– Noam Chomsky

Learning is by nature curiosity.

– Philo

There is no teaching until the pupil is brought into the same state or principle in which you are; a transfusion takes place; he is you and you are he; then is a teaching, and by no unfriendly chance or bad company can he ever quite lose the benefit.

— Ralph Waldo Emerson

It is that openness and awareness and innocence of sorts that I try to cultivate in my dancers. Although, as the Latin verb to educate, *educere,* indicates, it is not a question of putting something in but drawing it out, if it is there to begin with… I want all of my students and all of my dancers to be aware of the poignancy of life at that moment. I would like to feel that I had, in some way, given them the gift of themselves.

— Martha Graham

Learning without thought is labor lost; thought without learning is perilous.

— Confucius

A man who is pleased when he receives good instruction will sleep peacefully, because his mind is thereby cleansed.

— Buddha

It is better to know nothing than to learn nothing.

— Hebrew Proverb

In teaching children we must seek insensibly to unite knowledge with the carrying out of that knowledge into practice.

— Immanuel Kant

In seed time learn, in harvest teach, in winter enjoy.

— William Blake

And gladly would ye lerne, and gladly teche.

— Geoffrey Chaucer

In searching for the fundamental principles of the science of teaching, I find few axioms as indisputable as are the first principles of mathematics. One of these is this, He Is The Best Teacher Who Makes The Best Use Of His Own Time And That Of His Pupils. For Time is all that is given by God in which to do the work of improvement.

– Emma Hart Willard

The important thing is not so much that every child should be taught, as that every child should be given the wish to learn.

– John Lubbock

If a man keeps cherishing his old knowledge, so as continually to be acquiring new, he may be a teacher of others.

— Confucius

The successful teacher is no longer on a height, pumping knowledge at high pressure into passive receptacles.... He is a senior student anxious to help his juniors.

— Sir William Osler

If you have knowledge, let others light their candles at it.

— Margaret Fuller

The teacher is engaged, not simply in the training of the individual, but in the formation of the proper social life.

I believe that every teacher should realize the dignity of his calling, that he is a social servant set apart for the maintenance of proper social order and the securing of the right social growth.

I believe that in this way the teacher always is the prophet of the true God and the usherer in of the true kingdom of God.

— John Dewey

What people need and what they want may be very different…. Teachers are those who educate the people to appreciate the things they need.

— Elbert Hubbard

The future of the nation is on the shoulders of teachers and how they teach kids; the future of the world is in the classroom where the teachers are. And if we have any chance to guarantee a positive bridge to the 21st century, it is how we educate the children in the classrooms today.

— Richard Reginald Green

Teaching seems to me beyond doubt the greatest of the professions.

— Theodore Brameld

The best teacher will be he who has at his tongue's end the explanation of what it is that is bothering the pupil. These explanations give the teacher the knowledge of the greatest possible number of methods, the ability of inventing new methods, and, above all, not a blind adherence to one method, but the conviction that all methods are one-sided, and that the best method would be the one which would answer best to all the possible difficulties incurred by a pupil, that is, not a method, but an art and talent.

– Leo Tolstoy

Education has for its object the formation of character.

– Herbert Spencer

The best method for a given teacher is the one which is most familiar to the teacher.

— Leo Tolstoy

There is no such whetstone, to sharpen a good wit and encourage a will to learning, as is praise.

— Roger Ascham

Teaching should be such that what is offered is perceived as a valuable gift and not as a hard duty.

— Albert Einstein

Educator's Pledge

I accept not only the responsibility to instruct my students, but the responsibility to take advantage of the opportunity to stimulate and excite young people educationally.

I accept the responsibility to encourage my students to believe in themselves, and I will do this by helping them to develop specific awareness of the power that each one of them possesses to determine their own destiny.

I will challenge my students to reach just beyond that point where they are comfortable, so they will discover that their own perceptions of their potential are not their true limits.

As I set challenging tasks and goals before my students, I will guide them through the specific steps that will enable each one to reach these goals. This setting of high standards and giving the proper guidance to achievement will enable my students to become aware of their <u>true</u> potential, which is, through step-by-step discipline and hard work, to go beyond what they ever thought possible.

I will take advantage of the opportunity to guide my students to a concrete understanding of their own abilities:

➻ to question, rather than to just accept what they are told,

➻ to seek answers, when there are no simple solutions,

➻ to seek to understand, when true understanding requires grappling and wrestling with difficult concepts and ideas,

➻ to reason, using their own minds as sources of original thought,

➻ and to become contributors to, rather than just partakers of, the well-being of the world in which they live.

My educational goal is the **empowerment** of my students.

— Barbara H. Wagner

Much have I learned from my teachers, more from my colleagues, but most from my students.

— Talmud: *Ta'anith, 7b*

The bad teacher's words fall on his pupils like harsh rain; the good teacher's, as gently as the dew.

— Talmud: *Ta'anith, 7a*

Education makes a man a more intelligent shoemaker, if that be his occupation, but not by teaching him how to make shoes; it does so by the mental exercise it gives, and the habits it impresses.

— John Stuart Mill

The true teacher defends his pupils against his own personal influence. He inspires self-trust. He guides their eyes from himself to the spirit that quickens him. He will have no disciple.

— Amos Bronson Alcott

Any piece of knowledge which the pupil has himself acquired — any problem which he has himself solved, becomes, by virtue of the conquest, much more thoroughly his than it could else be. The preliminary activity of mind which his success implies, the concentration of thought necessary to it, and the excitement consequent on his triumph, conspire to register the facts in his memory in a way that no mere information heard from a teacher, or read in a schoolbook, can be registered.

— Herbert Spencer

Education is not the filling of a pail, but the lighting of a fire.

— William Butler Yeats

All of our teachers: how bright in our mind,
We recall every one, as they came;
Each, like a wise monarch, unselfish and kind,
Did make our advancement their aim.
Think not that the scholar, ne'er valued thy care;
Thy teachings sank deeper than thou wert aware.

— Priscilla Jane Thompson

For rigorous teachers seized my youth,
And purged its faith, and trimmed its fire,
Showed me the high, white star of Truth,
There bade me gaze, and there aspire.

— Matthew Arnold

To teachers, students are the end products, — all else is a means. Hence there is but one interpretation of high standards in teaching: standards are highest where the maximum number of students — slow learners and fast learners alike — develop to their maximal capacity.

— Joseph Seidlin

I can easier teach twenty what were good to be done, than be one of the twenty to follow mine own teaching.

— William Shakespeare

The man who can make hard things easy is the educator.

— Ralph Waldo Emerson

Part of teaching is helping students learn how to tolerate ambiguity, consider possibilities, and ask questions that are unanswerable.

— Sara Lawrence Lightfoot

Education is the ability to listen to almost anything without losing your temper or your self-confidence.

— Robert Frost

As teachers, we invest a great deal of our professional, intellectual lives trying to see beneath the surface of what we encounter. What drives our curiosity is trying to understand core phenomena or motivations that give rise to what we see. That is, we try, even if we don't always succeed, to be attentive and insightful learners.

– Roald Hoffmann and Brian Coppola

Teachers and learners are correlates, one of which was never intended to be without the other.

– Jonathan Edwards

To be a teacher in the right sense is to be a learner. Instruction begins when you, the teacher, learn from the learner, put yourself in his place so that you may understand what he understands and in the way he understands it.

— Søren Kierkegaard

It is a luxury to learn; but the luxury of learning is not to be compared with the luxury of teaching.

— R. D. Hitchcock

He who constantly aids children to their ends, hourly provides them with the satisfaction of conquest, hourly encourages them through their difficulties and sympathizes in their successes, will be liked; nay, if his behavior is consistent throughout, must be loved.

— Herbert Spencer

We should not be speaking *to*, but *with*. That is second nature to any good teacher.

— Noam Chomsky

Any teacher can study books, but books do not necessarily bring wisdom, nor that human insight essential to consummate teaching skills.

– Bliss Perry

We don't know one millionth of one percent about anything.

– Thomas A. Edison

Teachers learn from their students' discussions.

– Rashi

The aim of education should not be to teach how to use human energies to improve the environment, for we are finally beginning to realize that the cornerstone of education is the development of the human personality, and that in this regard education is of immediate importance for the salvation of mankind.

— Maria Montessori

In teaching, we do not impose our wills on the student, but introduce him to the many mansions of the heritage in which we ourselves strive to live, and to the improvement of which we are ourselves dedicated.

— Israel Scheffler

Only the brave should teach. Only those who love the young should teach. Teaching is a vocation. It is as sacred as priesthood; as innate a desire, as inescapable as the genius which compels a great artist. If he has not the concern for humanity, the love of living creatures, the vision of the priest and the artist, he must not teach.

— Pearl S. Buck

The essence of education is not to stuff you with facts but to help you discover your uniqueness, to teach you how to develop it, and then to show you how to give it away.

— Leo Buscaglia

Teaching Is
a Lifelong Journey

To teach is to touch the lives of many
and to help us learn life's lessons.
But to teach <u>well</u> is to make a difference
in all the lives you touch.

To teach is to be a parent, nurse, friend,
  and confidant;
to be a supporter, a leader, and a motivator.
But to teach <u>well</u>
  is to be all of these things,
yet not lose sight of who you are.
You share a part of yourself
with all whose lives
you have touched.

To teach is to be tender,
loving, strong, and giving
to all who rely upon you;
to encourage and praise.
But to teach <u>well</u>
is to believe in what
and whom you teach.

A teacher comes to master
  these many jobs
throughout the years.
But those who teach <u>well</u>
recognize that there
will always be more
to learn in life's journey,
and they never hesitate
to strive to learn it.

– Donna Bulger

A teacher who can arouse a feeling for one single good action, for one single good poem, accomplishes more than he who fills our memory with rows and rows of natural objects, classified with name and form.

— Johann Wolfgang von Goethe

Good teaching is one-fourth preparation and three-fourths theatre.

— Gail Godwin

You go into an audience and ask people to go back over their childhood and pick out the teachers that did the most for them. I think you will find in every case that they will say such and such a teacher waked them up, or such and such a teacher first inspired them. They will put it in different ways. They may have forgotten whether she was a good disciplinarian or not. The mechanical teachers will not be the ones they will speak of; it will be the teachers that roused them, that got hold of them. That means the teacher that found out the mental trait that was uppermost in the pupil, and that succeeded in giving it intellectual nutriment in such a way as to make it grow. The child did not know this trait. The other teachers did not find it out; but through some natural instinct, this particular teacher divined what was going on in that mind and succeeded in making connections.

That is the great object of education.

– John Dewey

Education should never work against a person's destiny, but should achieve the full development of his own predispositions. The education of a man today so often lags behind the talents and tendencies which his destiny has implanted in him. We must keep pace with these powers to such an extent that the human being in our care can win his way through to all that his destiny will allow — to the fullest clarity of thought, the most loving deepening of his feeling, and the greatest possible energy and ability of will.

This can only be done by an art of education and teaching which is based on a real knowledge of man.

— Rudolf Steiner

Both teaching and rational inquiry,
at their creative and inspired best,
thus lead us to the very threshold of
ultimate mystery and induce in us a
sense of profound humility and awe.

— Theodore Meyer Greene

As teachers we must believe in change, must know it is possible, or we wouldn't be teaching — because education is a constant process of change. Every single time you "teach" something to someone, it is ingested, something is done with it, and a new human being emerges.

— Leo Buscaglia

Teachers are like flowers:
they spread their beauty
throughout the world.
Their love of learning
touches the hearts of their students,
who then carry that sense of wonder
with them wherever they may go.
Teachers, with their words of wisdom,
awaken the spirit within us all
and lead us down the roads of life.

— Deanna Beisser

A Message of Thanks to All the Great Teachers in This World

Thank you for being such wonderful teachers, exemplary role models, and caring people. Thank you for knowing your subjects and sharing your knowledge. Thank you for not being afraid to treat students like real people. Thank you for showing acceptance, approval, and appreciation. These are all gifts that are so important to a student's development and that your students will always remember, just as they will also remember you.

Words of encouragement, a little respect, and simple gestures of kindness from a teacher promote the perfect climate for students to study, learn, and grow. Your attitude translates into a spirit of friendliness and good will toward others in a sometimes unfriendly world. Progress is easier in an atmosphere of creative freedom, joy, and ease, and you foster this feeling in your classroom.

I salute the good work you've done. I appreciate the people you are, and I thank you for your positive influence. You have passed on invaluable instruction and wisdom and created pleasurable moments associated with learning that will always be sweet memories.

Thank you for answering the call to be teachers. Thank you for the enduring impression you've made in the lives you have touched. Every community needs people like you. Your contributions are immeasurable. Your lessons are permanent. You improve our world. You are so important.

— Donna Fargo

Teaching is a process of becoming that continues throughout life, never completely achieved, never completely denied. This is the challenge and the fun of being a teacher — there is no ultimate end to the process.

— Frances Mayforth

Education is not a preparation for life; education is life itself.

— John Dewey

The teachers of this country, one may say, have its future in their hands.

— William James

God Bless the Teacher

God bless the teacher...
For in your care each day,
you teach the children
to laugh and play and enjoy
their lives that are
still unspoiled by a world
that is sometimes hard to understand.

God bless the teacher...
You build your students'
hopes and dreams and self-esteem.
You teach them compassion, friendship, and loyalty.
You help them grow and teach them things
that matter most.
You teach them how to be themselves.

God bless the teacher...
For being there
to calm your students' fears,
cheer them up, and dry their tears.
Thank you for everything you do.

— Julia Escobar

ACKNOWLEDGMENTS

We gratefully acknowledge the permission granted by the following authors, publishers, and authors' representatives to reprint poems or excerpts from their publications.

Random House, Inc. for "I touch the..." by Christa McAuliffe from I TOUCH THE FUTURE: THE STORY OF CHRISTA MCAULIFFE by Robert T. Hohler. Copyright © 1987 by Random House, Inc. All rights reserved. Reprinted by permission.

Wayne State University Press for "It is the supreme..." by Albert Einstein, "How to tell..." by Lascelles Abercrombie, "To be a..." by Søren Kierkegaard, and "Only the brave..." by Pearl S. Buck from QUOTABLE QUOTES ON EDUCATION by August Kerber. Copyright © 1968 by Wayne State University Press. Reprinted by permission.

Dutton, a division of Penguin Putnam, Inc., for "Teaching is one..." from LETTERS OF AYN RAND edited by Michael Berliner. Copyright © 1995 by The Estate of Ayn Rand. Introduction copyright © 1995 by Leonard Peikoff. Used by permission.

Alfred A. Knopf, Inc. for "No man can..." from THE PROPHET by Kahlil Gibran. Copyright © 1923 by Kahlil Gibran, renewal copyright © 1951 by Administrators C.T.A. of Kahlil Gibran Estate, and Mary G. Gibran. All rights reserved. Reprinted by permission.

Doubleday, a division of Bantam Doubleday Dell Publishing Group, Inc., and Faber & Faber, Ltd. for "The good teacher..." from THE JOURNALS OF SYLVIA PLATH edited by Ted Hughes. Copyright © 1982 by Ted Hughes as Executor of the Estate of Sylvia Plath. For "It is that openness..." from BLOOD MEMORY by Martha Graham. Copyright © 1991 by The Estate of Martha Graham. All rights reserved. Reprinted by permission.

The MIT Press for "It is a general..." from LANGUAGE AND PROBLEMS OF KNOWLEDGE: THE MAGNA LECTURES by Noam Chomsky. Copyright © 1988 by Massachusetts Institute of Technology. All rights reserved. Reprinted by permission.

The University of Michigan Press for "In teaching children..." from EDUCATION by Immanuel Kant, published by Ann Arbor Paperbacks. Copyright © 1960 by Ann Arbor Paperbacks. All rights reserved. Reprinted by permission.

Johnson Publishing for "The future of..." by Richard Reginald Green from EBONY MAGAZINE. Copyright © 1988 by Ebony Magazine. All rights reserved. Reprinted by permission.

Teachers College Press for "Education has for...," "Any piece of...," and "He who constantly..." by Herbert Spencer from HERBERT SPENCER ON EDUCATION edited by A. M. Kazamias. Copyright © 1966 by Teachers College, Columbia University. All rights reserved. Reprinted by permission.

The New York Times for "Teaching should be..." by Albert Einstein from THE NEW YORK TIMES, October 5, 1952. Copyright © 1952 by The New York Times Co. All rights reserved. Reprinted by permission.

Southern Illinois University Press for "What the teacher..." by Karl Menninger, "To teachers, students..." by Joseph Seidlin, "Any teacher can study..." by Bliss Perry, and "Teaching seems to..." by Theodore Brameld from AND MERELY TEACH by Arthur E. Lean. Copyright © 1968 by Southern Illinois University Press. Reprinted by permission.

National Science Teachers Association Publications for "As teachers..." by Roald Hoffmann and Brian Coppola from THE JOURNAL OF COLLEGE SCIENCE TEACHING. Copyright © 1996 by National Science Teachers Association, 1840 Wilson Boulevard, Arlington, VA 22201-3000. All rights reserved. Reprinted by permission.

Regnery Publishing, Inc., for "The aim of..." from EDUCATION AND PEACE by Maria Montessori. Copyright © 1972 by Mario M. Montessori. All rights reserved. Reprinted by special permission.

The Harvard University Press for "In teaching, we..." from "Philosophical Models of Teaching" by Israel Scheffler, HARVARD EDUCATIONAL REVIEW 35:2 (Spring 1965) p. 143. All rights reserved.

The Felice Foundation for "The essence of..." and "As teachers we..." from LIVING, LOVING & LEARNING by Leo Buscaglia, Ph.D., published by Ballantine Books. Copyright © 1982 by Leo F. Buscaglia, Inc. All rights reserved. Reprinted by permission.

Random House, Inc. for "Good teaching is..." from THE GOOD WOMAN by Gail Godwin. Copyright © 1974 by Gail Godwin. All rights reserved. Reprinted by permission.

South End Press for "We should not..." from POWERS AND PROSPECTS: REFLECTIONS ON HUMAN NATURE AND THE SOCIAL ORDER by Noam Chomsky. Copyright © 1996 by South End Press. All rights reserved. Reprinted by permission.

Gale Research, Inc. for "One looks back..." by Carl Gustav Jung, and "Part of teaching..." by Sara Lawrence Lightfoot. Taken from GALE'S QUOTATIONS edited by Shelly Dickie. Copyright © 1995 by Gale Research, Inc. All rights reserved. Reproduced by permission.

PrimaDonna Entertainment Corp. for "A Message of Thanks to All the Great Teachers in This World" by Donna Fargo. Copyright © 1999 by PrimaDonna Entertainment Corp. All rights reserved. Reprinted by permission.

Barbara H. Wagner for "Educator's Pledge." Copyright © 1999 by Barbara H. Wagner. All rights reserved. Reprinted by permission.

Julia Escobar for "God Bless the Teacher." Copyright © 1999 by Julia Escobar. All rights reserved. Reprinted by permission.

A careful attempt has been made to trace the ownership of poems and excerpts used in this anthology in order to obtain permission to reprint copyrighted materials and give proper credit to the copyright owners. If any error or omission has occurred, it is completely inadvertent, and we would like to make corrections in future editions provided that written notification is made to the publisher:

BLUE MOUNTAIN PRESS, INC., P.O. Box 4549, Boulder, Colorado 80306